D1135372

EVANGELISTIC PREACHING

Proclaiming the gospel to
non-Christians who are listening

EVANGELISTIC PREACHING

10 Publishing
a division of 10ofthose.com

ROGER CARSWELL

First published in Great Britain in 2015

British Library Cataloguing in Publication Data
A record for this book is available from the British Library

ISBN: 978-1-910587-17-1

Designed & typeset by Pete Barnsley (Creative Hoot)
Cover image copyright: http://www.tagxedo.com
Printed in the UK by CPI Group (UK) Ltd, CR0 4YY

10Publishing, a division of 10ofthose.com
9D Centurion Court, Farington, Leyland, PR25 3UQ, England

Email: info@10ofthose.com
Website: www.10ofthose.com

Dedication

To United Beach Missions,

Who have taught me so much about preaching the gospel to all ages

and types of people. I thank God for your ongoing commitment to

proclaiming the gospel to non-Christians who are listening, and your

training of numerous others to do the same.

Acknowledgements

I am grateful to all those who have helped me in the process of learning to preach: those who encouraged me as a teenager to grow as a Christian, and to preach on 'a soap box' in the open air, or on a beach mission. I am thankful that people have opened doors of opportunity for me to speak at events and services which they had carefully set up. My appreciation goes to those who have showed great patience, correcting my mistakes and nurturing my methods.

My family – parents, wife, and children – have been extremely understanding in not only allowing me to be away from home so much each year, but praying for me and encouraging me in the work.

With regard to this book, my deep thanks go to those who have read it, commented and criticised, improving my attempts to convey what I so passionately believe. I am especially grateful to Warren Wiersbe of Lincoln, Nebraska; Paul Windsor of the Langham Partnership; Peter and Pim Claridge of Cuckfield; Janice Bowman from the FIEC; Michael Orr from Cumbria; and my wife, Dot.

10Publishing has been helpful and encouraging throughout the process of writing and publication.

My deepest gratitude goes to my Lord and Saviour, Jesus Christ, without whom I would be lost and without hope. God, by His Holy Spirit, has written truths on my heart, which are very precious to me. His love is such that I long for every preacher to be determined to know nothing except Jesus Christ and Him crucified, and I pray that this book will encourage and equip us to do so.

Brethren, my heart's desire and prayer to God for Israel is that they may be saved. For I bear them witness that they have a zeal for God, but not according to knowledge. For they being ignorant of God's righteousness, and seeking to establish their own righteousness, have not submitted to the righteousness of God. For Christ is the end of the law for righteousness to everyone who believes.

... 'The word is near you, in your mouth and in your heart' (that is, the word of faith which we preach): that if you confess with your mouth the Lord Jesus and believe in your heart that God has raised Him from the dead, you will be saved. For with the heart one believes unto righteousness, and with the mouth confession is made unto salvation. For the Scripture says, 'Whoever believes on Him will not be put to shame.' For there is no distinction between Jew and Greek, for the same Lord over all is rich to all who call upon Him. For 'whoever calls on the name of the Lord shall be saved.'

How then shall they call on Him in whom they have not believed? And how shall they believe in Him of whom they have not heard? And how shall they hear without a preacher? And how shall they preach unless they are sent? As it is written:

'How beautiful are the feet of those who preach the gospel of peace,
Who bring glad tidings of good things!'

But they have not all obeyed the gospel. For Isaiah says, 'Lord, who has believed our report?' So then faith comes by hearing, and hearing by the word of God.

Romans 10:1–4 and 8–17

a soul winner's hymn

With a soul blood bought and a heart aglow,
Redeemed of the Lord and free,
I ask as I pass down the busy street,
Is it only a crowd I see?
Do I lift my eyes with a careless gaze,
That pierces no deep down woe,
Have I nought to give to the teeming throng
Of the wealth of the love I know?

Let me look at the crowd as my Saviour did,
Till my eyes with tears grow dim:
Let me look till I pity the wandering sheep,
And love them for love of Him.

As I read in the gospel story oft
Of the Christ who this earth once trod,
I fancy I see His look on the crowd,
That look of the Son of God;
He saw not a number in might and strength,
But a shepherdless flock distressed,
And the sight of those wearied, fainting sheep
Brought grief to His loving breast.

Dear Lord, I ask for the eyes that see
Deep down to the world's sore need,
I ask for a love that holds not back,
But pours out itself indeed;
I want the passionate power of prayer,
That yearns for the great crowd's soul,
I want to go among the fainting sheep
And tell them my Lord makes whole.

Mrs R.A. Jarvie (Young Life Hymns)

Contents

The need for evangelistic preaching

'The quest of man is met by the Word of God. The need of man is met by the activity of God. The sin of man is met by the forgiving love of God. And between man, with his need and his sin, and the Word of God in His mighty activity and His redeeming love stands the Christian preacher.'

– F.D. Coggan

When Andrew Neil resigned as the editor of *The Sunday Times* in 1994, he commented, 'I have been a journalist now for the last twenty years, and I have chronicled the decline of a nation.'

An American actor recently spoke of his love of London, 'It's great to be in a city going down the tubes in such style.' Whatever we think of recent legislation, media manipulation, educational emphases and populist trends, we have to ask ourselves how much of the spiritual declension and moral collapse in our land is due to reasons which can be laid at the feet of evangelicals. A root cause of our problems is that in recent years there has been a famine in our land – not of food or drink, but of the word of God. People are left as sheep without a shepherd, and are ignorant of basic Bible truths (cf. Numbers 27:17, 1 Kings 22:17 and Zechariah 10:2). It is time for those of us who love the Lord and His gospel to be fired up, then to fan the flames of evangelistic passion. We need to ensure that everyone is hearing the gospel proclaimed winsomely and faithfully. We are to proclaim in complete dependence upon God to use our words. Before every sermon I preach, I pray, 'Lord, without You I can do nothing, therefore will You please accomplish that which counts for eternity through this message?' Only God can 'give the increase'.

True evangelistic preachers are preachers of the word of God. They are the mouthpiece of the Bible, the word of God, to a lost world, pointing to God's decisive act in sending Jesus into this world for our salvation, which He procured through His death and resurrection. So they are not people just with something to say, nor preachers who have to say something, but proclaimers of the gospel who have something to say, and *have* to say it. In that sense, evangelistic preaching is truly prophetic, because it is preaching God's word to men and women who desperately need to hear it. Evangelistic preaching is the natural result of, indeed the overflow of, God's love. The life-giving, altogether loving God desires to

2

give His life and love to all. And it is in preaching that God speaks, acts, produces faith and saves people.

Sermons are the bridges we build bringing the word to the world. Human opinion is not worthy of comparison with the word of God, so all human thinking and religious tradition needs to be brought into line with God's truth. And human need will not be met by human resources or consensus but by the work and word of God. John Stott coined the phrase 'double listening' to encourage us to listen to and be aware of the thoughts and attitudes of those around us, as well as being saturated in God's word. Evangelistic preaching is not about conveying good advice or Christian opinions, but about the good news, which is God's message to humanity. The 17th-century puritan, Thomas Goodwin, had for some time set out to be a 'celebrity preacher' with clever insights of human wisdom. But when taking over from Richard Sibbes at Holy Trinity Church, Cambridge, he was told by Sibbes, 'Young man, if ever you would do good, you must preach the gospel and the free grace of God in Christ Jesus.' And that is what he did, to great effect.

Listening to sermons today?

It has almost become a mantra that today people cannot listen to a monologue, so sermons should be very short and snappy. Such thinking reflects more on the preacher than the hearer. We must not excuse poor, listless preaching about so marvellous a subject. In September 2014, an estimated 100 million people across the globe listened for hours to Judge Tholkozile Masipa handing down her verdict on Oscar Pistorius at his murder trial. Her delivery was hardly gripping, but the subject was enthralling. Ours is the most gripping, thrilling message in the world, plus we are handling the word of God, empowered by the Holy Spirit Himself. People can listen and will where we speak faithfully of Jesus with passion, clarity and love.

Of course, there is a cost to this. Proclamation of the gospel, which will include declaring some unpalatable truths, is both spiritually and emotionally draining. Richard Baxter's famous saying, 'Preach as a dying man to dying men', inevitably involves a giving of oneself that uses human energy and emotion, so we will need to prepare ourselves for this by spending time with the Lord, building up our inner, spiritual resources. We need to look at and linger over the Bible not only to prepare messages but to prepare ourselves as the messengers. Those who wait on the Lord will renew their strength. In waiting on the Lord, we pray for holiness and power, as well as for the Holy Spirit Himself to use the proclaimed message.

In days of increasing apathy, antagonism and hostility to the gospel, across the whole spectrum of society, it is tempting to hide behind Bible study, books and computer screens, vital though each are. I have a sneaking suspicion that we are spending far less time involved with eyeball-to-eyeball evangelism than we are seated behind our laptops and PCs. Such escapism is not going to move the world and bring men and women to faith in Christ. We need the courage to challenge people compassionately with the claims of Christ. Computers, useful as they are, so far have been unable to communicate emotion. They do not weep over the lost, and they are not the best means of spreading God's gospel, which should be taken and offered by God's people, in person, to every individual.

Phillips Brooks, the 19th-century American preacher, defined preaching as 'truth through personality'.[1] Preaching is more than teaching, though both are vital. Preaching aims not only to instruct the mind but also to move the will so that there is response to the message proclaimed. Evangelistic preaching includes three elements: teaching, testifying and persuading (see Acts 17:3–4 and 28:23). It means that we teach the basic truths of the word of God and the work of Jesus, we testify to its power in our lives and we seek to persuade (not manipulate!) people to come to Christ. 'Persuade' is a frequently used word in the New Testament, and need not be something to shy away from, as long as the persuader is acting in dependence on God, with respect for the people with whom they are communicating, and not demeaning the gospel or themselves.

The early Christians spread the gospel by word of mouth; we can learn from the commitment and pattern of life of those early believers:

- 'Day after day, in the temple courts and from house to house, they never stopped teaching and proclaiming the good news that Jesus is the Christ' (Acts 5:42).
- 'Those who had been scattered preached the word wherever they went' (Acts 8:4).
- 'When they arrived at Salamis, they proclaimed the word of God in the Jewish synagogues. John was with them as their helper' (Acts 13:5).
- 'Then Philip opened his mouth, and beginning at this Scripture, preached Jesus to him' (Acts 8:35).
- 'Paul… reasoned with them from the Scriptures, explaining and proving that the Christ had to suffer and rise from the dead' (Acts 17:2–3).
- 'From morning till evening he explained and declared to them the kingdom of God and tried to convince them about Jesus from the Law of Moses and the Prophets' (Acts 28:23).
- 'Although I am less than the least of all God's people, this grace was given me: to preach to the Gentiles the unsearchable riches of Christ, and to make plain to everyone the administration of this mystery …' (Ephesians 3:8–9).

- 'Surely you remember, brothers, our toil and hardship; we worked night and day in order not to be a burden to anyone while we preached the gospel of God to you' (1 Thessalonians 2:9).
- '… preaching the gospel of God to you free of charge?' (2 Corinthians 11:7).

It is passages like these that form the foundation to C.H. Spurgeon's words, 'If sinners will be damned, at least let them leap to hell over our bodies; and if they will perish, let them perish with our arms about their knees imploring them to stay … If hell must be filled, at least let it be filled in the teeth of our exertions, and let not one go there un-warned or un-prayed for.'[2] It seems that much of our Christianity today is stifling our responsibility to reach the lost with the gospel. Our frequently changing emphases have replaced reaching the unconverted with teaching the saints. It is good to have conferences for believers, but there is a need to prioritise events where the aim is to preach the gospel to those outside of Christ. 'But … if our gospel is veiled, it is veiled to those who are perishing, whose minds the god of this age has blinded, who do not believe, lest the light of the gospel of the glory of Christ, who is the image of God, should shine on them' (2 Corinthians 4:3–4).

Faithful, relevant proclamation

Genuine believers are concerned that there should be faithful gospel proclamation. We want to earnestly contend for the faith, just as much as an engaged girl protects her engagement ring from theft or loss, because it is so valuable and precious. If evangelism is preaching the gospel to non-Christians who are listening, then without being smug or proud, each gospel preacher will want to become an expert in evangelistic preaching. As we listen to and read what others are preaching, there will be either great joy, or deep concern about what is being proclaimed. And as life throws different experiences at us, we learn to minister to those who lives have also been roller-coasters of joys and sorrows. God never wastes any pain, or tears, toil or time. Everything that happens to us will be used to communicate this precious message engagingly and effectively.

This is not merely of academic intrigue. It has an impact on all of us who are concerned that the message of the cross would once again spread throughout the land. A century ago, the Student Volunteer Missionary Union defined evangelism as, 'The presentation of the gospel in such a manner to every soul in this world, so that the responsibility for what is done with it shall no longer rest upon the Christian church or any individual Christian, but shall rest upon each man's head for himself.' For that to be done there has to be fervent, relevant, prayerful evangelism, which means there must be faithful proclamation. Enthusiasm is sometimes read as evangelism, but evangelism, which undoubtedly should be enthusiastic, has to have in it a particular content. There can be no evangelism without a faithful evangel.

Despite the pressure on the evangelical community to be silent, or to at least modify our message, we have more opportunities than we can take to present the gospel. Let us learn from the apostle Paul to redeem every opportunity to explain the gospel and put the claims of Christ before the listeners. According to the book of Acts, Paul spoke about the Lord:

- In the synagogues (at least 10 times – see 9:20; 13:4–5; 14:1; 17:2, 10–17; 18:4 and 19:8)

- In the stately house of the proconsul Sergius Paulus on Paphos (13:7)

- At a prayer meeting by the river in Philippi (16:13ff)

- In a prison cell (16:31)

- In a market-place (17:17)

- At the Areopagus in Athens (17:22–31)

- In the homes of Titius Justus (18:7) and Priscilla and Aquila (18:26)

- In the lecture hall of Tyrannus in Ephesus (19:9)

- To the rioting crowd at Ephesus (22:1–21)

- Before the Sanhedrin at Ephesus (23:1–6)

- In the palace of Felix (24:25)

- In the court before Festus, Agrippa and Bernice (26:1–29)

- On the deck of a sinking ship (27:25)

- Under house arrest in Rome (28:23–31)

Writing in the *Evangelical Times*, William Payne said, 'It may surely be claimed that the Christian church was born of preaching. The Master Himself early identified preaching as one of the main concerns of His coming: "Let us go somewhere else to the towns nearby, in order that I may preach there also; for this is what I came for." (Mark 1:38)'[3]

Preaching is not only a privilege, but also a responsibility. Preachers have been entrusted with good news and have an indebtedness to God, as well as to their hearers. We are 'servants of Christ and stewards of the mysteries of God. Moreover it is required in stewards that one be found faithful' (1 Corinthians 4:1–2). That picture of the preacher is repeated in Colossians 1:25 and 1 Peter 4:10. We will have to give account to God as to how we have discharged our responsibility. Bishop Gore (1613-19) used to give his final charge to ordinands by saying, 'Tomorrow I shall say to you, "Wilt thou? Wilt thou? Wilt thou?" But there will come a day to you when Another will say to you, "Hast thou? Hast thou? Hast thou?"'

As we proclaim the gospel, we do so knowing that God's heart is towards men and women. They may be His enemies but His deep love desires them to come to Him: "'As I live," says the LORD God, "I have no pleasure in the death of the wicked, but that the wicked turn from his way and live. Turn, turn from your evil ways! For why should you die, O house of Israel?'" (Ezekiel 33:11). God wants people to be saved; He is 'not willing that any should perish but that all should come to repentance' (2 Peter 3:9). Evangelistic preachers will feel, to a much lesser extent than did our Lord, the hurt and emotional pain of seeing people reject the truth. When we know this grievous agony of heart, we are experiencing a little of 'the fellowship of His sufferings' (Philippians 3:10). Jesus looked over His beloved capital and longed for them to be gathered to Him: He wanted to, but they were not willing. The eternal destiny of men and women depends on their response to Jesus, so we will love the lost and point them to the Friend of sinners. In our proclamation of the gospel, we pray that the Holy Spirit will take hold of His holy word and apply it to unholy hearts to make them more like Jesus.

chapter 1

Evangelistic preaching focuses on Christ and Him crucified

'John did no miracle, but all things that John spake of this man were true. And many believed on Him there. John 10:41–42.'

– The words engraved on the gravestone of evangelist W.P. Nicholson, in Bangor, N. Ireland

When the apostle Paul wrote his evangelistic book, which we call the Letter to the Romans,[4] he makes the focal point the cross of Christ. Romans 1 describes humanity in the raw; Romans 2 describes refined humanity, then Romans 3 describes religious humanity, but 3:23 concludes that they are all sinful. Then Paul explains how God devised the means whereby we who should be banished from Him might be reconciled to Him. It is through Christ and Him crucified. Every individual and every religion, even atheism, leads to God, because every individual is going to meet God one day! Only Jesus leads to God on the throne of grace; all other religions lead to God on the throne of judgement. After Paul's explanation of what Jesus accomplished by His death on the cross in Romans 5, Paul examines the consequences and application of His death and resurrection. It is arguable that the whole book of Romans is about Christ, His cross and resurrection, explaining why Jesus was crucified and rose again, what was achieved at Calvary, and its impact and claims on us, the nations and history.

When Paul wrote explaining his method and motivation in preaching – his homiletic – which we read in the beginning of 1 Corinthians, he builds up to the climactic conclusion in 2:2 that he determined or resolved 'not to know anything among you except Jesus Christ and Him crucified.' A definite Christ and a definite cross led him to that definite conclusion: that in evangelistic preaching he was always going to pave the way to Christ crucified. Interestingly, John Stott, preaching at the Keswick Convention in the year 2000, spoke on the early chapters of 1 Corinthians. His outline of the passage 1:17 to 2:2 had three points:

1. God's power through weakness in the evangel (1:17–25)

2. God's power through weakness in the evangelised (1:26–29)

3. God's power through weakness in the evangelist (1:30–2:2)

12

Paul later wrote, 'Moreover, brethren, I declare to you the gospel which I preached to you … For I delivered to you first of all that which I also received: that Christ died for our sins according to the Scriptures, and that He was buried, and that He rose again the third day according to the Scriptures …' (1 Corinthians 15:1-4). The Greek word *euangelizimai* means 'to announce good news' and is used over fifty times in the New Testament, and the word *kērussō* meaning 'to be a herald', or 'to proclaim', is used more than sixty times. Other words used in the New Testament mean 'to talk', or 'to discourse', or 'to tell thoroughly', but all convey how prominent for the early Christians was the work of declaring the good news of Jesus crucified and risen to the people of their generation.

The basics of the gospel message

Examining in detail the sermons preached in the book of Acts (though it is evident that what we have in Acts are sermon outlines or précis, or they would have all been very short messages indeed), every one of them refers both to the resurrection of Jesus and to repentance. There has to be death before there can be resurrection, and there has to be the cross if repentance is to be of any value. Belief in the resurrection made Christian preaching possible, and repentance gave Christian preaching its objective.

The whole gospel is contained in Jesus, and through the gospel we see the very heart of God more clearly than through creation alone. Gospel proclamation has to focus on what God has done through Jesus, and an explanation of the hidden work of Christ on the cross. God laid on Him the sin of the world. 'For He made Him who knew no sin to be sin for us' (2 Corinthians 5:21). Jesus, the righteous One, died for we who are unrighteous, and His righteousness can be imputed to us. He was made sin; He carried it all on Himself. The blood of Jesus was shed so that we might be justified, redeemed, and reconciled to God. 'He Himself is the propitiation for our sins, and not for ours only but also for the whole world' (1 John 2:2). Through His death and resurrection we are adopted into the family of God and so may call God our Father. The person of Jesus is the very heart of the gospel. No wonder we often read in Wesley's Journals words like, 'I offered Christ to the people for three hours'. It is clear that we cannot overlook or omit the big themes of the gospel and expect to see genuine conversions to Christ.

Jesus spelled out in His final words – reported by Luke in his gospel – what is to be the content of an evangelistic message. We read that Jesus told them, 'This is what is written: The Christ will suffer and rise from the dead on the third day, and repentance and forgiveness of sins will be preached in his name to all nations, beginning at Jerusalem' (Luke 24:46–47). God's agenda for the church is that we proclaim to our neighbours and the nations Jesus' sufferings, His resurrection, the need to repent and the promise of forgiveness. In fact Jesus says that this is what all the Scriptures are about – see verses 44–45. So there is no difference in emphasis between the Old and the New Testament. There are common, central themes, and at the heart of them is the idea of redemption purchased by Jesus on the cross. Salvation and forgiveness of sins are one and the same in the Bible. Whatever else we are doing, if we are not proclaiming Christ crucified and risen, whilst at the same time calling people to repent and believe, we are not preaching evangelistically. Ajith Fernando writing about Matthew 24:14 ('This gospel of the kingdom will be proclaimed throughout the whole world as a testimony to all nations, and then the end will come'), says this verse is important 'because it presents what should be the most important agenda in the church's programme: the taking of the gospel to the whole world.'[5]

After Jesus' great commission in Luke 24, He assures that the Triune

God is committed to the gospel being proclaimed to our neighbours (i.e. Jerusalem) and the nations. He says, 'Behold, I send the Promise of My Father upon you; but tarry in the city of Jerusalem until you are endued with power from on high' (24:49). So, we have the promise of the Father, the plans of the Son, and the power of the Spirit, working with us (Mark 16:20), as we work with Him (1 Corinthians 3:9).

The priorities of Christian communication

It is noble and good to give porridge to the poor, to save the whale, for street pastors to provide flip-flops for drunken revellers, to teach agriculture and provide irrigation systems for the developing world, to be environmentally friendly as well as to create and serve the community. Such endeavours may even be used to build a bridge to people so that we can tell them about Jesus, but these are not what gospel ministry is about. Of course, kindness and good deeds will characterise the Christian. We want to do good – it comes naturally to the believer (Ephesians 2:10). But the great commission is to go and tell, to preach and proclaim, to warn and welcome sinners as we introduce them to Christ. Topping the agenda of church leaders' and members' meetings ought always to be strategically reviewing and planning the programme of fulfilling Jesus' words before His ascension. It is a priority of the church and of our preaching. There are some helpful seminars today on why churches die. One obvious reason is that evangelism has fallen from the top of priorities for church.

Newspapers recently reported that churches in the last year have provided 10 million 'man hours' to local authorities to help them in times of financial cuts. If local councils ask us to run youth clubs and care for the needy, praise God, but only if they are happy for us to present the gospel and speak about Jesus. I read recently, 'Sometimes people talk as if by renovating a city park or turning a housing slum into affordable, liveable apartments, we are extending God's reign over that park or that neighbourhood … but the kingdom isn't geographical. Rather, it is defined relationally and dynamically; it exists where knees and hearts bow to the King and submit to Him … Good deeds are good, but they don't broaden the kingdom of God.'[6] The evangelical's calling is not 'community' but Christ in all things having the pre-eminence. If schools, universities or social gatherings do not want us to speak of Jesus, then let us not water down the message, simply to 'keep our toe in the door'. One of the most devastating criticisms I heard about a well-known preacher who had just spoken at a university CU carol service was, 'Great communicator … no gospel!'[7]

I remember discussing these issues on a beach mission when I was a teenager. The imaginative team leader made up a parable to illustrate the truth as he saw it. He told the story of a man rescued from drowning at sea. But, in saving the drowning man the rescuer was battered by the waves and beaten against the rocks. Eventually, he was airlifted by a helicopter to a hospital where it was unsure as to whether he would live. Some weeks later the person rescued went to see his 'saviour' who was still in the Intensive Care Unit. They talked for a while during which time the hospitalised man offered his visitor a Polo mint. When eventually he left his hospital visit, he bumped into a friend who enquired where he had been.

'To see someone in hospital,' he replied.

'Well, are you going to tell me who it was?' he was asked.

'Oh, just a friend!'

'Well, who?' he was asked again.

The answer came: 'Oh … just someone who once gave me a Polo mint!'

Of course, there is something incongruous about that. What is a Polo mint compared with being rescued from drowning, especially when it cost the rescuer so much? The beach mission leader was warning against the danger of sermons and testimonies that are focused on the 'Polo mints' of the peace, joy, purpose, friends and sense of well-being we have found since becoming Christians, rather than forgiveness and reconciliation with Jesus purchased at such a great price. We are not offering more joys to the unbeliever, but different joys. Paul wrote, 'For Christ did not send me to baptize, but to preach the gospel, not with wisdom of words, lest the cross of Christ be made of no effect' (1 Corinthians 1:17).

Evangelistic exposition

I have been asked on a number of occasions, by people concerned to be true to the Bible text, how they can proclaim the cross if it isn't actually directly written in the passage that is being expounded. It is a valid question underlining the desire to let the Bible speak for itself. I answer the question by pointing out that the whole of the Bible has Christ and Him crucified as its backcloth, its emphasis and its purpose. Every passage is to be preached in the context of the whole of the Bible. The Bible has been given to reveal God to us, and to make us wise unto salvation. If we are faithfully to proclaim a biblical gospel to unconverted people, the finished work of Jesus will be central. That doesn't mean that we simply 'bolt on' the cross to our sermons, leading to the message following a formula, but rather as Christopher Ash, of the Cornhill Training Course, puts it, that we seek 'to see how the lines of scripture point to Christ and His cross in ways that are persuasive and convincing'. There are so many themes to be developed and proclaimed in the cross of Jesus that gospel preaching need never be dull or repetitious.

The cross is the demonstration of God's love and grace. Yet there is a strange reluctance, almost embarrassment, to make clear what was

17

happening when Jesus was crucified. There is nothing more important than that people everywhere should hear and understand the gospel. There is no place for complacency that demonstrates a lack of urgency to 'rescue the perishing'. The great 19th-century evangelist D.L. Moody found this out in a way that was to change his ministry. After preaching the gospel he sent his congregation away asking them to consider what he had said, and told them that the next week he would explain how to become a Christian. He was unaware that that very night the Chicago Fire would take many of their lives. Urgency and love characterised his preaching after that.

Some months ago, I went to a large evangelistic meeting in the north of England. The American speaker had been interviewed on radio, and by the major serious newspapers. The event was well advertised, a good crowd attended and the speaker was engaging, intelligent, well-thought-through and gentlemanly. He spoke for 50 minutes to a mixed group including people from other religions. However, although this was an 'evangelistic' meeting, he didn't once mention Jesus, the cross, or other essentials of the gospel. Aspects of the gospel did come through later, when Christians in the audience pressed the evangelist to explain our message. No Muslims asked any questions, but when I reflected on this, I realised that they would actually have agreed with all that was said. Later, I heard the chairman defend this non-proclamation of Christ, arguing that we shouldn't be preaching 'Christ and Him crucified' because people are so far back in their understanding that we have to convince them first of God's existence. This is hardly the approach of Scripture, or the method of the evangelists in Acts. Paul Windsor of the Langham Partnership says we should not preach 'synagogue sermons' but Christ-centred ones. A truly Christian sermon is one that would cause you to be thrown out of a synagogue (or a mosque), which of course is exactly what happened to the early Christian preachers.

We should be 'always ready to give an answer for: 'Always be prepared to give an answer ... for the hope that [we] have' (1 Peter 3:15). Apologetics, which explains and recounts the evidences for why we believe what we believe, has its place, but actually, 'the reason for [our] hope' is Jesus, His death and resurrection. We have good reasons to believe in God, the Bible, Jesus, the validity of Christian conversion, etc. but whilst boldly declaring the historical facts on which we base our faith, let us explain what our faith is, in whom our faith is placed, and what Jesus has accomplished for us. I am glad when people believe in God, recognising that He is not a delusion, but that isn't enough – even demons acknowledge God's existence. Our emphasis must always be John 3:16: 'For God so loved the world that He gave ... ' otherwise the gospel message will be lost and the proclamation of the God of the Bible will become weak and woolly. To quote D.L. Moody, 'The main thing is to keep the main thing the main thing.'

Apologetics or gospel?

I am not sure that people today are actually asking the questions we like to answer anyway. Maybe 30 years ago the ordinary non-Christian was interested in whether there is evidence that Jesus rose from the dead, but it isn't the issue which concerns people outside the church today. In a society where many feel that they have few cares and that they can live for the moment for pleasure and materialism, where awareness of the Bible and the Christian faith is dwindling, proclaiming the message that Jesus brought is therefore totally counter-cultural. Christ and Him crucified is still a stumbling block to some and foolishness to others, but there are still those in our self-centred world to whom it is startling news.

It is not sufficient to simply believe in God. We need the gospel to know what God is like; otherwise in a fallen world, people could picture a false, a fallen god. Martin Luther wrote: 'If you ask, "what is the gospel?" no better answer can be given than these words of the New Testament: "Christ gave His body and shed His blood for us for the forgiveness of sins." Charles Spurgeon expressed the same idea when he said, 'I build my study on Mount Calvary.'

In every evangelistic message I deliberately go over certain basic truths, which are absolutely vital ingredients to an understanding of the message. I will speak a little about the character of God (often briefly explaining the doctrine of the Trinity); I talk about our sinfulness and the fact that there is judgement and that we deserve punishment; I preach about Jesus, particularly explaining His death and resurrection; I emphasise the need to repent and believe the gospel; and I always refer to heaven and hell Dr Francis Schaeffer, founder of the L'Abri Community, said at the Lausanne Congress on World Evangelisation in 1974, 'We must say, if evangelicals are to be evangelicals, we must not compromise our view of Scripture. There is no use of evangelicalism seeming to get larger and larger, if at the same time appreciable parts of evangelicalism are getting soft at that which is the central core, namely the Scriptures.'

If our efforts to bring people to faith meet with no success and we do not reap the desired fruit, we should nonetheless continue to lovingly warn, admonish, proclaim, plead and pray. If people accept the gospel, we rejoice. If they do not accept it, it grieves us, but we are to continue to proclaim the gospel, praying that our loving God will continue to pursue the hearer in His own special way. With a heart for the Lord and for the lost people around us, we must speak the gospel with the worthy motive of hoping that people will be converted. Preachers are sometimes urged to scratch where people itch, but it is our responsibility under God first to try to get people to itch in the right places, then to point them to the remedy.

I smile at the story of Sir Alec Guinness who was involved in acting the part of a Roman Catholic priest whilst filming in France. At the end of a day, he was returning to his hotel, still dressed in his robes and clerical collar. A little boy innocently ran up to him and put his little hand in Sir Alec's with the words 'Mon papa!' Together they walked for a while, before going their separate ways. The little boy no doubt felt secure, but he was deluded. I fear the same consequences occur when we are preaching a cross-less 'gospel'. In evangelistic preaching God, through the Holy Spirit, speaks, acts and stirs up faith, thus adding to the church. God uses the words of His people. But if we try to find the source of our message only in ourselves, our intellect or our ability, our proclamation will become merely an expression of the spirit of the age. We must not be as chameleons reflecting the colour of the environment, but Christians radiating the fullness of the glory of Christ. John Calvin said, 'When the minister executes his commission faithfully by speaking only what God puts in his mouth, the inward power of the Holy Spirit is joined with his outward mouth.'

chapter 2

Evangelistic preaching manifests love

'To love to preach is one thing, to love those to whom we preach is quite another.'

– Francis of Sales

I know little or nothing about John Watson, except that he was a 19th-century Scottish theologian who said to fellow preachers, 'Be kind, you do not know what battles people are fighting.' It is one of two statements which has most impacted the way I seek to share the gospel. It is not for us to preach the gospel in a way which displays no love for the listeners. D.L. Moody is said to have 'loved them in'. And someone commented on the 19th-century Scottish preacher Robert Murray M'Cheyne that his denunciations of sin were so terrible because they were so tender. 'Preaching should break a hard heart, and heal a broken one,' was said by John Newton who had experienced both. Jesus was moved with compassion as He saw the crowds as sheep without a shepherd. And looking over Jerusalem, which had killed the prophets and was shortly to crucify Him, He exclaimed, 'How often I wanted to gather your children together, as a hen gathers her chicks under her wings, but you were not willing!' (Matthew 23:37). The apostle Paul, echoing the love of Moses centuries earlier, said he would have traded his own eternal relationship with God if only his nation could have been saved. Of course, only Jesus could actually bring salvation, but it is a Christ-like love, which shows such a willingness to sacrifice oneself for the needs of others.

Those who listen to us are not our enemies. They are as we once were. And we want them to be as we are. The gospel offers new life to everyone, even if they do not want it. The Bible plainly teaches that God 'is patient … not wanting anyone to perish, but everyone to come to repentance' (2 Peter 3:9). The evangelistic preacher will reflect that desire: we want everyone to repent and believe the gospel. Our vocabulary is not 'You sinners!' but 'We sinners!' Rather than being angry at the sinfulness of those to whom we proclaim, we are to show non-patronising pity for this lost generation. I am always challenged by the socialist William Morris who commented that whenever he saw a drunk he felt deeply for him. The greatest act of friendship is to introduce someone to Jesus Christ, so we are to lovingly tell people about Him, and gently bring them nearer to Him. This takes time, and yet we are always aware of the urgency there is for people to trust Christ. When Samuel Wilberforce became Bishop of Oxford, he made a resolution 'never to hurry men who come to consult you'. The care of souls is not only the duty of a pastor but also of the evangelist. There is a great need to display wisdom in helping people come to new birth in Christ.

Whilst there is so much in society that upsets Christians, nevertheless we are not called primarily to be protesters, but proclaimers of good news. I praise God for the boldness of the Old Testament prophets, as they spoke the word of God, denouncing specific national sins, and urging repentance on the princes, the priests, the prophets and the people. I am not an Old Testament prophet, rather a preacher of the gospel. I am one sinner telling another sinner of the wonderful Saviour who 'able to save to the uttermost those who come to... Him' (Hebrews 7:25). I try to speak as simply and plainly as possible. I am to feed sheep, not giraffes, so I don't want my vocabulary to go over people's heads. John Wesley tested his sermons out on kitchen maids to ensure that everyone would be able to understand what he was saying. Humility of life and language should mark out evangelistic preachers.

Those who don't want to hear the gospel

Speaking personally, I think I may have ceased preaching long ago if it were not for the call of God on my life as a Christian, and the love of Christ, which constrains me. His love for me, and my pale reflection of love for Him, is such that I will love those whom He loves. If God

Himself loves the world of lost people, it is inevitable that I will too. The unambiguous ingratitude of the majority of the people I am trying to reach, towards the truths of the gospel, is disheartening. I want everyone to be saved, and I will work as any slave towards that end, but I know that most people don't want what I have to share. Jeremiah repeatedly warned his people that they were refusing to listen to the words of God. The same is true today. As we have seen before, Jesus looked over His capital city of Jerusalem and cried from His innermost being, 'O Jerusalem, Jerusalem … How often I wanted to gather your children together, as a hen gathers her chicks under her wings, but you were not willing!' (Matthew 23:37). So following Jesus' example, let our proclamation come from a heart of love, so that we speak with tenderness, and act with compassion. If our hearts are full of love we will find that it is hard – though not impossible – to offend people. To keep a heart of love we need time to be alone with the Lord, and also time with ordinary people. We will become disconnected with real needs if we are not daily rubbing shoulders with unconverted people. All preachers need to be in meaningful contact with the people who choose not to listen to them publicly preaching, if they are to reach *all* their locality with the gospel.

We are to speak from the inmost passion of our heart, but to do so with winsome care, recognising that people have been wounded by the society in which they live, and blinded by the enemy of their souls. In Mark 1 we are told that 'Jesus came … preaching' (v. 14), then in Mark 12:37 we read that 'the common people heard Him gladly'. And in Luke 4 we are given a possible reason why. They wondered at 'the gracious words which proceeded out of His mouth' (v. 22). Love, sympathy, care, understanding, compassion, tenderness and just being winsome should be characteristics of the evangelist. We read of Stephen in Acts

6:10 that 'they could not stand up against his wisdom or the Spirit by whom he spoke'. Clearly, both what he said and the way he said it made a powerful impact on his audience.

Pastoral evangelism

There is a pastoral element in all gospel ministry, even that of the evangelist, which demonstrates genuine interest in the many needs of the people we long to reach with the gospel. Understanding something of the suffering of Christ, we also are to be aware of the sufferings of people. Warren Wiersbe, whilst a voracious reader, says that he has learned more from the bedsides of those whom he is visiting than from all the books he has read. There are lessons to be learned from both activities, but evangelists must beware of declaring truth in a manner which undermines the very message that is being proclaimed. Peter, the preacher, cut off the ear of the High Priest's servant, but many evangelists have cut off the ear of their would-be listeners by something foolishly said or done!

However, we are not at liberty to choose our message. The gospel we preach has been committed to us and it is for us to proclaim God's word faithfully. Clearly that means that we are under an obligation to be true to all the Scriptures and not only the more palatable themes. The Bible is plain-speaking; it is not a code where certain words do not mean what they so obviously appear to mean. God means what He says and says what He means. Preachers, and indeed their hearers, are warned against only teaching truths that taste sweet. It is worth regularly reading the whole of Jeremiah 23, but verses 16–18 summarise the chapter: 'Do not listen to what the prophets are prophesying to you; they fill you with false hopes. They speak visions from their own

27

minds, not from the mouth of the LORD. They keep saying to those who despise me, "The LORD says: You will have peace." And to all who follow the stubbornness of their hearts they say, "No harm will come to you." But which of them has stood in the council of the LORD to see or to hear his word? Who has listened and heard his word?'

Hell and judgement

Whilst the subject of hell is not dwelt on in the evangelistic messages of the book of Acts, judgement is a clear, underlying theme. We cannot simply gloss over Matthew 5:22, 8:12, 13:50, 18:9, 22:13, 25:41, 46, Mark 9:43–48, Luke 12:5, 16:19–31, John 3:16–21, 36, 5:29, Romans 1:18, Ephesians 2:3, Philippians 3:19, 2 Thessalonians 1:9, Jude 7, 13, Revelation 14:9–11, 19:20 or 20:1–15. Jesus was most tender-hearted: He who loved the most, warned the most, and for us it is a dereliction of our calling not to warn people of impending judgement and possible punishment. We should do so with tears in our eyes and meekness of spirit. There will be tangible meekness and certainly no flippancy, for as ambassadors of God and knowing the terror of the Lord, we will so want to urge people to repent and believe. John Stott wrote in his book *Between Two Worlds*:

I constantly find myself wishing that [today's] preachers could learn to weep again but either our tear-springs have dried up or our tear-ducts have become blocked. Everything seems to conspire together to make it impossible for us to cry over lost sinners who throng the broad road which leads to destruction. Some preachers are so preoccupied with the joyful celebration of salvation that they never think to weep over those who are rejecting it. Others are being deceived over the devil's lie of universalism. Everybody will be saved in the end, they say, and nobody will be lost. Their eyes are dry because they have closed them to the awful reality of eternal death and outer darkness of which both Jesus and His apostles spoke. Yet others are faithful in warning sinners of hell, but do so with a glib and even a sick pleasure, which are almost more terrible than the blindness of those who ignore or deny its reality.

chapter 3

Evangelistic preaching demonstrates creativity

'He is the best speaker who can turn the ear into an eye.'

– Arabian proverb

Warren Wiersbe has been pastor of three churches in the USA before becoming the director of *Back to the Bible* Broadcast. He a is most engaging communicator. Anything he has written is worth reading! In his book *Teaching and Preaching with Imagination*, written for seminary students, he develops the theme of the value of creativity in biblical preaching, and in so doing gives an insight into what it is that has undergirded the thinking behind his own preparation and preaching. Wiersbe goes through every book of the Bible showing how God used imagination to convey truth, and it is an exposition of the statement: 'People's minds are not debating chambers but picture galleries; therefore speak so that you turn people's ears into eyes and they see the truth.'

That sentence has been a guiding principle in all my communication of the gospel. Someone said, 'The common people are captivated more readily by comparisons and examples than by difficult and subtle disputations. They would rather see a well-drawn picture than a well-written book ... For teaching purposes it is useful to have comparisons and examples on hand; not only Paul, but also the prophets and Christ Himself, very often used them.'

This is not just a modern communication technique developed because we live in a post-modern age, or because we perceive that people are not able to concentrate on words alone for more than a few minutes. The fact that the Lord Himself uses metaphor, parable, illustration, poetry, imagery, or imagination surely gives us the role model to follow.

The apostle Paul allows us an insight into his preaching in Galatians 3. He first berates the Galatian believers from being diverted from straightforward trust in the finished work of Christ: 'But even if we, or an angel from heaven, preach any other gospel to you than what we have

32

preached to you, let him be accursed. As we have said before, so now I say again, if anyone preaches any other gospel to you than what you have received, let him be accursed' (1:8-9). Then Paul shudders at the thought that they may break into factious disunity. So he reminds them of what it was they first believed: 'O foolish Galatians! Who has bewitched you that you should not obey the truth, before whose eyes Jesus Christ was clearly portrayed among you as crucified?' (3:1).

The Galatians were not present when Jesus was actually crucified, so what does Paul mean by his question? Surely he is referring to his preaching. He used words in such a way that it was as if a picture was being painted for them so that it was as if the cross on which Jesus had been crucified was placarded before the listening Galatians. His message was centred on Christ crucified, but graphically they saw what Paul was saying, and by faith they received the offer of salvation.

It is too easy to regurgitate pat phrases when we should be tailoring the message for the person we are addressing. We need to avoid and overcome this tendency, and can do so by keeping our own minds fresh and informed. The painter Sir Joshua Reynolds said, 'The mind is but a barren soil; a soil which is soon exhausted, and will produce no crop, or only one, unless it be continually fertilised and enriched with foreign matter ... he who resolves never to ransack any mind but his own will soon be reduced from mere barrenness to the poorest of imitations; he will be obliged to imitate himself and to repeat what he has often before repeated.' Minds need to be constantly replenished with information and insights, stories and pictures, laughter and sorrow, news and ideas. This is particularly true if we are to be proclaimers who communicate effectively. There is nothing wrong with using the same messages over and over again – we have good precedents for so doing from John the Baptist, the Lord Jesus, and a host of others including John Wesley, who said that he didn't get into a sermon until he had preached it 40 times! But if we do so we must walk with God and preach so that the message comes across with fresh passion and earnest longing for the lost to be saved. Sometimes it is helpful to rework a sermon so that old truths come across with fresh relevance.

Open-air evangelism

I am convinced that open-air preaching is a vital way of keeping preachers in touch with reality as well as getting out the gospel to those completely outside the church. Preaching in the open air is also one of the finest ways to develop the skill of a preacher to gain and keep the attention of people who will listen to the word of God. If a preacher cannot keep a crowd in the open air, should he/she be expected to be a speaker asked to captivate an invited audience? If you can gather a few together I would encourage you to go into a precinct or park and winsomely to proclaim the gospel and share your testimonies.

I have found it a good help, too, to write and give away gospel tracts. This practice disciplines the evangelist to succinctly express great truths in a way which is engaging and understandable. Giving away these leaflets may well prove to be the key to either opening or closing the door of conversation about Jesus.

I will never forget a sermon which I never heard preached. My eldest son, however, did, and phoned me immediately to excitedly repeat what he had heard from Alistair Begg. He had preached on David and Goliath, but outlined his three points with John McEnroe's famous refrain, 'You cannot be serious!' Using that phrase, Alistair Begg pointed out that basically this is what David would have thought when he showed surprise to his brothers at their lack of military action against Goliath. Later, it was as if King Saul used the same words to David when he offered to go and fight the giant. David refused Saul's offer of armour – he didn't put his trust in heavy metal! But didn't Goliath more or less say the same when he saw young David approach him with merely a sling and stones? A creative and unforgettable outline was used to drive home the truth of God's word.

If the congregation fall asleep, wake up the preacher! Illustrations not only keep the attention and interest of the listener, they clarify what we want to say. C.H. Spurgeon said, 'Reasons are the pillars ... but similitudes are the windows which give the best lights. The chief reason for the construction of windows in a house is ... to let in light. Parables, similes, and metaphors have that effect; and hence we use them to illustrate our subject, or in other words, "to brighten it with light" (which is Dr Johnson's literal rendering of the word "illustrate").' Warren Wiersbe says, 'An apt quotation is like a key; it opens doors to new investigations of truth and new discoveries of living.' I have over twenty-five books of quotations and find them invaluable to stimulate my mind with new ideas and insights. I then use the quotation itself or paraphrase the idea in my messages.

The variety of listeners

Some of the people we want to reach are pleasant, kind, respectful, God-fearing and receptive to the message; others are simply unlovely, unlikeable, arrogant, rude, godless, selfish individuals. Some of our listeners are well educated, and have taken on board the world's philosophies, whilst others are ignorant of most things except the celebrity culture of today's society. Some are committed to religions where there is no concept of our loving God who gave Himself to redeem us, yet whose culture is bound together with their religion; others have no religious understanding at all. Some read quality newspapers, some scan the pictures of gossip magazines; others don't read at all, or if they do it is in a foreign language. A few have been to Sunday school, the vast majority have a view of Jesus picked up from a school teacher or television!

Our calling is to reach all of these, and also to equip other Christians for the same work of ministry, and so edify the body of Christ. We are to turn the eyes of people away from themselves and the world, so that they may look to God. To begin with, we have to make a connection from where we are to where they are, and then to take them to where they should be in relation to Christ. To do so, we have somehow not to make ourselves appear better than them, but to become all things to all people that by all means we may reach some with the gospel. And all the time, we must bear in mind that our dependence is not upon our skills and abilities in communication but upon God. John Stott said, 'The secret of preaching is not mastering certain techniques, but being mastered by certain convictions.' Deep convictions about the gospel will, though, encourage us to become experts in communicating those precious truths in a way that is accessible and interesting.

Without using jargon, which listeners do not understand, and yet being thoroughly biblical, we are to explain the gospel. Colin S. Smith in a chapter entitled 'Keeping Christ central in preaching' says, 'In the past … evangelism was rather like hanging washing on a clothesline that was already in place. You could take texts like John 3:16 or Romans 5:8 or Isaiah 53:4–6 and hang them on the "line" of a Judeo-Christian world view. The problem in trying to reach postmodern people is there is no clothesline … The great challenge before the preacher is to put up the clothesline.'[8] What does the average non-Christian understand by the words 'God', 'sin', 'born again' or 'repent'? Whilst using the words, we have to define them; whilst simplifying the gospel message, we have to keep its awesome nature and God-qualities. Archbishop Temple said of Bishop Ryle: 'The language of those sermons is perfectly simple, and simply perfect.'[9] It is good to have a plan or an outline in our minds, and normally this should be made clear to those listening so they can follow where we are going. I personally don't like projecting the outline on a screen though, believing that I am *preaching* rather than *teaching* the gospel. My message is not a lecture, which simply conveys information, but a declaration of the good news of Jesus, which looks for a response.

Our authority comes from preaching the Bible. It, and it only, is God's word, so we need to learn again the lesson of Billy Graham and say in effect, if not in actuality, what Billy so often said, 'The Bible says...' Learn to quote Bible verses accurately, then use them in your preaching, and you will see how much more powerfully your messages come across. Our jokes, illustrations, homilies might make an immediate impression, but only preaching the Bible will make an eternal impression. God loves to honour His Son and His word, and nothing will lead to blessing from God like preaching about Jesus from the Bible. This is exactly what Jesus did with the two on the road to Emmaus, and what Paul did with his visitors from morning to evening, in his prison in the city of Rome (see Acts 28:23–31).

chapter 4

Evangelistic preaching connects with the non-Christian

'A preacher is like a man who hears a call for help and drops everything to run to the rescue. He is intent on one thing and he gives himself fully to it. But when he spends five or ten minutes getting into his sermon, he is like a man pausing to visit an art gallery before diving into the ocean to save the drowning swimmer.'

– Warren W. Wiersbe

In Stuart Olyott's book *Ministering Like the Master* his first chapter is entitled, 'Jesus was not a boring preacher'. In striving to be relevant and engaging, I have heard so many who, whilst preaching what is true, do so without evangelistically expounding the Bible. If the gospel is 'foolish' to some, it is especially wise to make the word of God our only authority. Our aim, as evangelistic preachers, should be to preach the Scripture to unconverted people and proclaim the good news. It is the Bible, the word of God, that is to be the foundation of all we preach. What can be more thrilling than to read and then preach the Bible? It has always been relevant and interesting, but never more so than in an age when people do not know even the most basic Bible stories. God takes His word and by His Holy Spirit applies it to the minds and hearts of the hearers. The Scriptures make people wise to what is meant by salvation.

Evangelism is proclaiming the gospel to non-Christians who are listening. It cannot be evangelism if the gospel is proclaimed but no unbelievers are present to hear what is being preached. So, though I love the idea of a Sunday evening gospel service, if the unsaved are not present and listening, we will be reminding Christians of the wonderful gospel, but it may be that we are merely going through the motions without doing what we are supposed to be doing. I remember a cynic telling me that his church was celebrating its centenary, and then he added, 'Yes, we are celebrating keeping the gospel in these four walls for the last 100 years!' We must devise means whereby those who would not normally have an opportunity to hear do actually hear the word. We read of the early disciples that they 'went out and preached everywhere, and the Lord worked with them ... ' (Mark 16:20).

There are preachers who insist on a particular size of congregation before agreeing to preach. I question this attitude. The size of the congregation should not be the uppermost consideration. After all, Jesus opened the Scriptures to just two on the road to Emmaus and Philip was taken from the crowds in Samaria to evangelise the Ethiopian eunuch alone. In fact, Jesus made villages and towns His focal point of ministry, not the cities we regard as centres of influence. Our strategies may not be the same as His were. He never went to the 'movers and shakers' in the hope that His message would have a trickle-down effect. The apostle Paul, on the other hand, did go to the cities and, from them, reached out to the surrounding regions. My experience is that sometimes a small church consists of Christians who are earnest and prayerful in seeking to evangelise their locality, and I feel honoured to work with them.

We are under marching orders to proclaim the gospel to everyone. It is natural to think that the best use of our life is to work amongst the most receptive people. However, that may not be God's calling on us. Ezekiel was called as a young man, by the River Chebar in Babylon, to be a prophet to his people. As the Lord spoke to him the Spirit entered him and God revealed his life's work to him. He was to literally eat the scroll of God's word and proclaim it whether the people listened or refused to hear. God then said that if He had sent Ezekiel to a different people they would have listened, but instead he was to preach to a stubborn and hard-hearted people who were not willing to listen.

It is not many decades ago that Christians preached to cinema queues. If that is not appropriate for today, we have to think how we reach those totally outside the gospel circles in which we normally operate. Paul was not so aloof that he could not say, 'I have become all things to all men, that I might by all means save some' (1 Corinthians 9:22). The nightclub culture means that many people get up when I go to bed, and go to bed when I get up. But who reaches these tens of thousands of relatively young people with the gospel? And how can we effectively reach them? Who is getting alongside the people who live on tough sink estates? I praise God for courses like *Christianity Explored*, *Identity* and *Stranger on the Road to Emmaus* and have urged all the churches and universities where I take missions to follow up the evangelism with these word-based courses. I am glad too about the emphasis on doing one-to-one Bible studies through a Gospel. I have seen *The Word One to One* and *Uncover* used to great effect. But, let us not ignore the fact that the vast majority of people do not have Christian friends who could invite them to something like that. Courses are recommended but cannot be the only part of a church's evangelistic programme. An evangelistic programme leads into courses, and they in turn lead into an evangelistic programme. Keeping evangelism high on the agenda of the church includes ensuring that all classes, cultures and communities around us are being reached in a thorough way. Jesus said, 'Go into *all* the world and preach the gospel to *every* creature' (Mark 16:15, my italics).

A lost weapon in our armoury

Evangelistic preaching has become a lost weapon in the armoury of many churches, and 'evangelical' preachers often squander the opportunities that are given to them. I have never understood the mentality of ministers who decide, for example, in wedding sermons primarily to speak to the couple who are being married. Surely, they can be spoken with at other times, but the gathered congregation will comprise people who may never hear the gospel in another setting. Instead, there are many obvious wedding and marriage themes in the Bible which cry out to be the basis of evangelistic messages. The same can be argued for sermons preached at funerals, or around Christmas, harvest and, of course, Easter. Campbell Morgan said that the essentials of a sermon are truth, clarity and passion, and a crowd willing to listen to a message deserve a gospel presented with these ingredients.

These are opportunities which are handed to us on a plate, but we need to be creating opportunities to reach those who would not naturally find themselves in church. Work in the open air can be very effective, not only in reaching the lost, but in teaching young Christians how to reach the lost. I commend to you open-air preaching, as well as beach missions, youth camps, services in care homes and home-based evangelistic events. They can all be organised by a small group of Christians burdened to reach people who are either on the fringe of church activities, or a million miles from them. There is a cost to this, but sacrificial service is totally consistent with the pattern of Christ-like living. And younger Christians have their skills refined as they, perhaps timidly, begin the work of proclaiming the gospel in these more informal settings.

In evangelistic preaching we need to hear what we are saying with the ears of those who are actually hearing. We should put ourselves in the place of the listener. We are to listen as if we are the thoroughly exhausted mother-of-three; we are the one whose every contact with religion has been negative; we are the aspiring graduate seeking a life of success and happiness; we are the office worker living in a difficult home who also has a rather immoral boss; we are the struggling business person; or we are the despairing woman in her mid-50s who has just been given bad news from her doctor. We are to understand our hearers rather than only expecting them to understand us.

Many of our listeners will believe that God is a delusion; that science has disproved the Bible; that we as religious people are against everything; that our message is about what we should and should not do; that our religion is as good or bad as any other; and that there is no judgement or after-life anyway! They feel that we are only about telling them things, never about listening. Those we are trying to reach probably know very little of the Bible. Basic stories such as Noah, David and Goliath, Daniel in the lions' den or the work of Jesus are either unknown or regarded as myths on a par with Greek mythology. Our vocabulary is either unknown to them, or if the words are familiar, they are defined differently, so that 'God' is not understood as the God of the Bible, and 'sin' is not what God calls sin, and 'repentance' is simply a gobbledegook word. They need to know that what we are proclaiming is true, relevant and works.

Keeping the listeners' attention

Without appearing fanatical or eccentric we will want to use all our energy and enthusiasm to arrest and hold the attention of the hearers. Personally, I don't follow the practice to start with a joke or the inconsequential, though I will sometimes approach my subject from an angle. Rather, I want to convey the fact that I am in earnest about what I am proclaiming. I like the thought of Richard Hostetter of Winston-Salem Bible College in North Carolina who said, 'You will lose people's attention when you never use the rhetorical pause, vary your rate of speaking, or change your volume. No one pays attention to a droning aeroplane engine; but when the engine slows down, speeds up, roars and purrs, sputters, and even stops and starts during operation, it rivets the attention of all its hearers.'[10]

Most non-Christians are happy most of the time, and quite content to keep God on the fringe of their lives. He is perceived to be an irrelevance and an antiquated notion. Most people's religion is from the media, and God is kept at a distance. Of course, we will also encounter people who have sensitive or prepared hearts and want to come to faith, but don't know how. And there will be others who hear the gospel just once and are saved. Yet all people today will require that we show patience as we carefully explain the gospel story.

Around us are people who often think and act in ways that are profoundly ungodly. Our calling is not to denounce their waywardness, but to declare the gospel. When the apostle Paul viewed the idolatry of Athens his despair was overwhelming, but rather than condemning the people he simply proclaimed the risen Christ to them. The Christian community has come across as being mean and judgemental, yet our calling is to mission rather than admonition. Jesus must be the focus of our message to the people of our generation.

Whilst never changing the central themes of our message, we will have to adjust our approach to suit the people to whom we are preaching. George Wilson M'Cree was an open-air missioner of a bygone era. In his book *Highway Witnessing*, he said, 'I have preached under the sky to fishermen, miners, poachers, ship-carpenters, shepherds, masons, soldiers, railway men, labourers, shoemakers, costermongers, thieves, tramps, atheists and drunkards, and I know that there was a great difference between the audiences thus gathered together; and I have felt the necessity of adapting my words to the assembly which was before me, so as, if possible, to meet the wants of every soul there … A sermon which you might properly preach on the sands at Scarborough would be most improperly preached in Seven Dials in London.'

For us, it is to this generation we have been called to preach and proclaim the gospel. Wycliffe Bible translators popularised a chorus some years ago which began with the words, 'Every person, in every nation, in each succeeding generation has the right to hear the news that Christ can save.' And if we do not reach this generation with the gospel no one else will ever be able to – 'how shall they hear without a preacher?' Let us ask the Lord to search our hearts asking if we have grown stony-hearted in our responsibility to the lost around us.

chapter 5

Evangelistic preaching expects results

'It is our calling to persuade, and if it may be, to convince. That is not preaching which is not preaching for a verdict.'

*– Richard Roberts in
The Preacher as Man of Letters.*[11]

I remember reading in the Christian newspaper *Evangelicals Now* a review of an evangelistic book. The reviewer described herself as 'the wife of a pastor of a small Baptist church in Oxford'. She warmly commended the book with words like, 'an easy read', 'a good book', 'the gospel set out in a very clear and simple way', etc. Then she added, 'It is a shame the author saw the need to invite people to Christ, "praying this prayer" in the epilogue rather than letting the testimonies speak for themselves. While not being able to recommend the book wholeheartedly ... ' I was taken aback and thought, what has evangelicalism come to that a book written for non-Christians is reviewed by a fellow Christian and criticised because it invites people to come to Christ, and suggests a prayer they could pray to express their repentance and faith towards God?

We must never be guilty of imposing our theological systems on clear Bible passages. Nor must we allow fear of offending people to overshadow the God-given commands and stark warnings, as well as its glorious offer of hope, to present the gospel of Jesus to every person. The biblical text must never be misrepresented. Bishop J.C. Ryle pointed out that George Whitefield continuously applied his evangelistic messages: 'He was not content with sticking on a meagre tailpiece of application at the end of a long discourse. On the contrary, a constant vein of application ran through all his sermons.' Here is an extract from his sermon on Jeremiah 6:14: 'What is hell, but to be absent from Christ? If there is no other hell, that would be hell enough ... Get acquaintance with God, then, and be at peace. I beseech you ... that you would be reconciled to God. My business this morning, the first day of the week, is to tell you that Christ is willing to be reconciled to you. Will any of you be reconciled to Jesus Christ?'[12]

Generally speaking, our nation no longer knows the gospel. It bothers me that we are failing to get across the message of 'Christ and

Him crucified' (1 Corinthians 2:2), but even when we do, it is without the pleading with the hearers to respond, to repent, to believe, to come to Jesus. Was it only He who is permitted to invite people to 'Come … all you who labor and are heavy laden … ' (Matthew 11:28)? Was Peter making a mistake when he concluded his great sermon at Pentecost by urging his listeners to believe? He urged: 'Repent and be baptised, every one of you, in the name of Jesus Christ for the forgiveness of your sins. And you will receive the gift of the Holy Spirit. The promise is for you and your children and for all who are far off – for all whom the Lord our God will call' (Acts 2:38–39). Luke adds, 'With many other words he warned them; and he pleaded with them, "Save yourselves from this corrupt generation"' (Acts 2:40).

In fact, the appeals of God throughout the Bible are many. None of them involve doing anything but simply responding to God's gracious invitation, which is not in a vacuum, but is based on all that Jesus has done for us. People in Bible days, and today, are urged to:

- Come to Him (Isaiah 1:18 and Matthew 11:28–30)
- Look to Him (Numbers 21:4–9 and Isaiah 45:22)
- Believe on Him (John 3:16 and Acts 16:31)
- Receive Him (John 1:12)
- Repent (Acts 17:30)
- Call on Him (Romans 10:13)
- Choose Him (Joshua 24:15)
- Be saved by Him (Acts 2:40)
- Trust in Him (Psalm 115:9–11)

It is clearly wrong to have an 'appeal' without proclamation, but is it not equally wrong to have proclamation without 'appeal'? The gospel preacher is, under God, looking for the same results that Paul rejoiced about when he thought of the believers in Rome: 'you wholeheartedly obeyed the form of teaching to which you were entrusted' (Romans 6:17). We must not lose confidence in the ability of the Lord to use us to win souls to Christ. This would be a lack of faith in the promises of God. Psalm 126:6 says, 'He who goes out weeping, carrying seed to sow, will return with songs of joy, carrying sheaves with him.' We dare not be intimidated by the scorn of the world into a silence that dares not 'plead with men' (as it says of Bunyan on the plinth of his statue in Bedford). For there to be fruitfulness through our ministries it must be evident that there is an urgency about our message, and not a 'take it or leave it' attitude.

If it is hard to find such an 'appeal' in the sermons of Paul, it is probably because he was usually interrupted by his irate listeners howling for his blood or objecting to his words. But we repeatedly read that he explained (the gospel), testified (to the grace of God in his own life), and persuaded (people to repent and believe). It is this persuasive element in evangelism which conveys the pressing need for people to respond to the grace of God. Persuasion is not manipulation, which can occur when some distort the gospel by giving the impression that if only people will put up their hand, or say a particular prayer, they will be saved. The gospel is never to be manipulative, but neither is it to be presented so casually that we give the impression that it hardly seems to matter what people do with it. Billy Graham repeatedly said that everyone whom Jesus called, He did so publicly. Evangelistic preaching will give people the opportunity to respond to the gospel. But we are not to make up in the 'appeal' what is lacking in the sermon. In Jesus' Parable of the Great Banquet we read that some people were invited, some had to be persuaded and others compelled to come and dine (Luke 14:15–24). Evangelists often talk to a person once and once only, so we will want to explain the gospel and spell out how the listener can respond.

In Mark 1 Jesus appeared in Galilee. He was a familiar friend to those He met, but He spoke in such an authoritative way that:

- They left their vocation (v. 18), the livelihood which men usually cling to;

- They left their parents (v. 20), when family bonds in Jewish life were very strong; and

- They were prepared to leave the devil's chains (v. 24), representing a complete change of priorities.

Of course, evangelistic preaching includes sowing gospel seed as well as reaping a harvest of those who come to Christ. Some will have their first introduction to the Christian message at an evangelistic service and then will take steps to find out more and discover Jesus. The children's evangelist Hudson Pope said, 'Never plant a tree where a hole has not been dug.' The Lord is well able to save someone the first time they hear the gospel, but usually there is a process of ploughing the land, sowing and watering the seed before the harvest appears. Jesus made this clear in His parable: 'This is what the kingdom of God is like. A man scatters seed on the ground. Night and day, whether he sleeps or gets up, the seed sprouts and grows, though he does not know how. All by itself the soil produces corn – first the stalk, then the ear, then the full grain in the ear. As soon as the grain is ripe, he puts the sickle to it, because the harvest has come' (Mark 4:26–29).

Honesty and integrity

I think we are all aware of the temptation to exaggerate the success of our work. I could name several well-respected organisations that for the sake of 'marketing' their ministries so that they will receive greater support, exaggerate the numbers of 'responses'. This is dishonest and dishonouring to the Lord who we are claiming to serve. It is sin, and leads to cynicism amongst the more discerning. Nevertheless, in the Bible there is the book of Numbers! In Acts 1:8 Jesus instructed the early Christians to witness in ever-extending concentric circles. They were to start in Jerusalem (where Jesus had just been crucified), then Judea (where He had been opposed), then Samaria (to a mixed race and despised people group), then to the pagan, Gentile world. Within 30 years the gospel had reached the capital of the Roman Empire and there were believers in Caesar's palace. They had gone from the city, to the country and then the continent. Of course, there was opposition to what was being proclaimed. When Paul preached in Jerusalem, the religious capital, he was mobbed; when he preached in Athens, the intellectual capital, he was called 'a babbler' (Acts 17:18); when he witnessed in Philippi he was imprisoned; in Thessalonica he was chased out; and in Berea he had to be smuggled out. Anticipating his preaching in Rome he said, 'I am not ashamed of the gospel …' (Romans 1:16). However, the early work of the church was so effective that we have six progress reports in the book of Acts:

- 6:7 – 'the word of God spread, and the number of the disciples multiplied greatly in Jerusalem, and a great many of the priests were obedient to the faith.'

- 9:31 – the gospel had spread throughout Palestine, and Stephen had been martyred; 'the churches throughout all Judea, Galilee, and Samaria … [were] walking in the fear of the Lord and in the comfort of the Holy Spirit, they were multiplied.'

- 12:24 – Paul had been converted as had Cornelius, and the church had extended to Antioch; 'the word of God grew and multiplied.'

- 16:5 – the preaching of the gospel had gone throughout Asia Minor and Galatia; 'So the churches were strengthened in the faith, and increased in number daily.'

- 19:20 – Christianity had extended to Europe and the great Gentile cities; 'So the word of the Lord grew and mightily and prevailed.'

- 28:31 – Paul was now in prison in Rome; 'preaching the kingdom of God and teaching the things which concern the Lord Jesus Christ with all confidence, no one forbidding him.'

There is a reason for such expansion. The Christians were 'daily in the temple, and in every house, they did not cease teaching and preaching Jesus as the Christ' (Acts 5:42). The early Methodists had a similar attitude stating, 'You have nothing to do but to save souls, therefore spend and be spent in this work.'

James S. Stewart, in his book *Teach Yourself Preaching*, recalls one of the most remarkable scenes described in Tolstoy's *War and Peace*. Set in the Russian headquarters, a messenger brought to Kutuzov, the old commander-in-chief, the first news of Napoleon's retreat from Moscow. After the years of terrific strain and agony to which the Russians had been subjected, the tidings seemed incredible. After a long pause, when no words would come, the old man turned to the icons and without restraint cried, 'Great God! My Lord and Creator! Thou hast heard my prayer! Russia is saved!' And then he burst into tears. But the Christian gospel has greater tidings, which are more moving and wonderful than even the deliverance of a nation.

Let us pray for faithful, biblical, expositional, lively evangelistic preaching, which is proclaimed with confidence and conviction to unconverted people, who are listening. For that to be done, we must not allow ourselves to be constrained to use vocabulary or keep to a style which is designed to appeal to a particular evangelical peer group, so ensuring their approval. Evangelistic preaching is *ipso facto* preaching whose aim is to reach the lost, not to court the smile of our friends. We have authority in that we are messengers of God. D.L. Moody met tremendous opposition when he first preached in universities. He was persistently interrupted and scoffed at. At last Moody responded, 'You jeered at the hymns, and I said nothing. You jeered at the prayers, and I said nothing. But now you jeer at the word of God. I would as soon play with forked lightning!'

John Calvin said, 'The gospel cannot be proclaimed without driving the world to rage.' All who are involved in preaching the gospel will find opposition from the devil, the world and the wicked. And the clearer the presentation of the gospel, the greater will be the ferocity of the opposition. But as we struggle and feel the heat of this, we also find ourselves strengthened by the Lord Himself. Our message is going to be an aroma of life unto life to some, and an aroma of death unto death to others (see 2 Corinthians 2:15–16). We love and pray for those who oppose us, but we cannot temper and adjust our message to pacify their rage: 'For we are not, as so many, peddling the word of God; but as of sincerity, but as from God, we speak in the sight of God in Christ' (2 Corinthians 2:17). Political correctness is hardly an ingredient of the gospel message!

Our authority in preaching

We have an authority that no humanly devised theory can equal.

We are proclaiming what the mouth of the Lord has spoken. We need have no need for modesty or humility over God's word. It is more valuable than gold, expressing the heart of God, and His only remedy for individual's needs. Read carefully and sombrely Paul's words to Timothy, and digest the seriousness of our calling as preachers of the gospel: 'In the presence of God and of Christ Jesus, who will judge the living and the dead, and in view of his appearing and his kingdom, I give you this charge: Preach the Word; be prepared in season and out of season; correct, rebuke and encourage – with great patience and careful instruction' (2 Timothy 4:1–2).

Dr Martyn-Lloyd Jones' definition of preaching was 'logic on fire'. We need to pray that God Himself will be speaking through our preaching, and that it is His word which we are proclaiming. In gospel preaching there is no place for relying on self, or projecting oneself. James Denney said that a preacher cannot convey the impression both that he is a great preacher and that Jesus Christ is a great Saviour. Henry Ward Beecher said, 'Great sermons are nuisances. Show-sermons are the temptation of the devil!' Evangelistic preaching should never be simply pious neutrality, unimaginative, ill-prepared, and spineless. According to Romans 1:16, the gospel is not an idea to be debated or a philosophy to be discussed, but a power to be unleashed. There is a God-given authority when the Bible is being genuinely preached. If we are naturally humorous individuals, let us by all means be funny (in moderation), but let us remember that we are gospel people with an eternal message to share. And if we are not naturally humorous, let us not irritate our listeners by trying to be! We need to learn to be serious people who know how and when to be flippant, rather than flippant people who know how to be serious. One-time American pastor Al Martin said, 'A dear servant of God said to me, "You cannot be a clown and a prophet both. You have got to make a choice." I hope I have made the right choice. This does not mean we shall not be truly human and that we shall feel there is something sinful in the natural ability to laugh. But the unnatural effort to be a joker amongst our people must be done away with…' C.H. Spurgeon, like his Saviour, knew how to be very funny, but the abiding memory of him, like his Master, is that he was a very earnest, evangelistic, passionate pastor/preacher.

A true evangelistic sermon is an organised and concentrated presentation of the good news of Jesus so that people understand and potentially respond to the gospel. We preach, not dependent on the cleverness of our sermon material, but having our sufficiency in God; and we look to Him to use our words, so that they come across not as the words of men, but as they are in truth, the word of God. If we believe that God uses His word, then we will preach it faithfully rather than relying on our clever word-creations to convince people. It is the gospel – the message of Christ and His cross – that is so dear to the heart of God that He uses it to touch the hearts of people. Jesus came, not so much to preach the gospel but that there might be a gospel to preach. Nevertheless, we can learn from Him that He used a variety of introductions to reach different people; each person was unique, but all needed His forgiveness and newness of life. He had the perfect words for every occasion and individual. He was constantly seeking people, and to be with Him was to be at the centre of evangelistic action. He never used glib, repetitive catchphrases. Where Jesus was working, God the Father and the Holy Spirit were working.

As well as the Holy Spirit working, conscience is the evangelists' ally, so that people hearing the word also hear the whisper of conscience saying, 'That's right … you are a sinner.' Rabbi Duncan said that the belief in God presses in many and varied ways upon men and women.

But we need the Holy Spirit to convict the people, cross-examining them as they stand in the dock, so that not only do they feel their need, but also that they might desperately look for a way of escape, for freedom and forgiveness.

God uses His word and His Spirit to bring new life. For this, there must be both prayer and proclamation. Jesus exemplified this. In Mark 1:35 we read that Jesus rose in the morning, a great while before day, departing to a solitary place and there prayed. Three verses later we read that Jesus turned to His disciples saying that they must move to the next town to preach there also. Prayer and preaching are married together, and no one must put them asunder. These twin spiritual disciplines are illustrated in the incident when the delightfully maverick prophet Ezekiel was told to prophesy to a valley of dry bones. Most of us will be able to sympathise with the challenge! When asked by the Lord if those dry bones could live, he diplomatically replied, 'O Lord GOD, You know' (Ezekiel 37:3). Then he was commanded to prophesy to the bones. As he did, there was a rattling and bone came together to bone. The foot bone joined the anklebone; the ankle bone joined the leg bone; the leg bone joined the knee bone; and so on. Soon Ezekiel was surrounded by skeletons, before, beside and behind him. As he continued 'preaching', muscles, tendons, then flesh covered the bones, so that then all around him were corpses, an army of dead bodies!

Finally, God commanded Ezekiel to speak to the wind, the breath, the Spirit and, as he did, the corpses became filled with the wind, the breath, the Spirit, and they stood up, a mighty, living army. Of course, the immediate point to the passage is referring to the nation of Israel, but there is a principle here, which looks like a mathematical equation:

The word + the Spirit = new life or new birth.

So we preach, we proclaim, and as we do, we pray. And in doing so, we are looking to God to do His silent, convincing work of convicting people of their sin, pointing them to Jesus, and bringing them to faith in Him. This book is not about prayer, but prayer is vital if preaching is to be blessed and fruitful. I am convinced that where there are failures in ministry, the causes will find their root in prayerlessness. Believing prayer is not simply for preaching, but to be the daily pattern of the evangelist. Where there is such prayer, evangelistic preaching will usually, under God, precipitate a crisis in people's thinking. Our duty is to gain the ear and preach the gospel which the Holy Spirit uses to win the heart. And how encouraging it is to remind ourselves that the Holy Spirit authenticates what the preacher is saying. God Himself leaves the unbeliever convinced that what is being preached is true, and that they should respond. He drives home the truths that we are proclaiming, hence our sense of expectation that God will give the increase as we proclaim 'Christ and Him crucified.'

Let us remember that God uses the weakest Christian as well as the most powerful evangelist. He uses a tract, a sentence or a poster as a tiny seed, and then waters and nourishes the word until there is new birth. Read again Mark 4:26–29 which expresses this so encouragingly.

Whenever the gospel is preached in a way that exalts Jesus, it is as if He comes into the midst of those listening. There is a sense that He is moving amongst the listeners, resting His hand on the shoulders of the people there.

John Henry Jowett said, 'reaching that which costs nothing accomplishes nothing'. The preparation of both the life and the sermons of the proclaimer is all-consuming. It takes time and hard work to study and then to work at the messages so that they are faithful, engaging and earnest. This means that every aspect of life is focused on proclaiming

Christ and Him crucified to men and women. Richard Baxter said to fellow preachers, 'We are seeking to uphold the world, to save it from the curse of God, to perfect the creation, to attain the ends of Christ's redemption. And are these works to be done with a careless mind or a lazy mind or a lazy hand? O see that this work be done with all your might! Study hard for the well is deep.'

For me personally, this means that everything I read, listen to or watch – whether Christian or secular – feeds into my mind and life to be funnelled as fuel to communicate more effectively. I study, read and pray so that I may be like the Lord Jesus whom I love, and then make Him known to all around me – people He loves and for whom He gave Himself. I am bought with the blood of Jesus, and therefore am not my own. My desire is that every bit of me, all that He has given me, would be wholly His and used to bring others to Christ. When I read the lives of Christians who have gone before, and willingly sacrificed their all in order to reach the lost, I will gladly pour out my life for Jesus. He is worth it! And we are called to be watchmen on the ramparts of the world. Like sentinels we are to keep vigil over the men and women around us. There is something wrong if we preach to lost men and women the greatest news in the world in a way that is dull, listless and lacking in a heart-felt passion. This is the most important message in the world so we cannot be apathetic. Neither must we be over the top, but if we come from time with the Lord, to making Him known, our hearts will be on fire, and our love for the hearers will be self-evident.

Some preachers have something to say, and others just have to say something. A real evangelist is someone who has something to say, and has to say it. And that 'something' is absolutely vital! There must be a burdened longing to proclaim the good news of Jesus. As missionary Henry Martyn said, 'Here let me burn out for God.' We read of the apostle

Paul that he 'devoted himself exclusively to preaching' (Acts 18:5). He told Timothy to: 'Preach the Word ... in season and out of season' (2 Timothy 4:2). Is there any greater privilege, joy and responsibility? So, let's go to it and preach Jesus faithfully to our needy, hurting, godless world!

References

1 His imposing statue in Boston has him standing, preaching, with his arm in the air, and behind him is Jesus, with His hand resting on Brooks' shoulder.

2 C.H. Spurgeon, 'The wailing of Risca' sermon, 349 New Park Street pulpit, December 9, 1860.

3 *Evangelical Times*, 'Whatever happened to preaching?', February 1995.

4 Paul had not yet visited the city of Rome, though he knew of the church there. He wrote to ensure that they had truly understood the gospel of grace. He wrote with the desire that those early Roman believers might be clear as to the Christian message.

5 Ajith Fernando, *Jesus Driven Ministry* (IVP, 2003), p. 123.

6 Taken from a highly recommended book, *What is the Mission of the Church?* by Kevin DeYoung and Greg Gilbert (Crossway, 2011).

7 See my chapter with that as a title in *The Thinker*, (Authentic Media, 2006).

8 Taken from *Telling the Truth: Evangelizing Postmoderns*, ed. D.A. Carson (Zondervan, 2009).

9 I recommend J.C. Ryle's *Expository Thoughts on the Gospel* (Banner of Truth, 1987), as a very helpful foundation for evangelistic sermons which are based on the four Gospels.

10 Taken from *Learning from Great Preachers* by Arthur Reynolds, (Avon Books, 1997).

11 Richard Roberts, *The Preacher as Man of Letters* (LLC, 2011).

12 Taken from *Select Sermons of George Whitefield* (Banner of Truth, 1958), p. 94.

Recommended books

I commend these titles for developing an evangelistic ministry:

- *And Some Evangelists*

  by Roger Carswell (Christian Focus Publications, second edition 2014)

- *Christian Leaders of the 18th Century*

  by J.C. Ryle (Banner of Truth, new edition 1978)

- *The Dynamics of Preaching*

  by Warren Wiersbe (Baker Book House, 1999)

- *Lectures to My Students*

  by C.H. Spurgeon (Christian Focus Publications, 2008)

- *Listening to the Giants*

  by Warren Wiersbe (Baker Book House, 1979)

- *Memoirs and Remains of Robert Murray M'Cheyne*

  by Andrew Bonar (Banner of Truth, 1966)

- *Ministering Like the Master*

  by Stuart Olyott (Banner of Truth, 2003)

- *Moody: A Biography*

  by John Pollock (Revell 1997)

- *A Passion for Souls: The Life of D.L. Moody*

  by Lyle Dorsett (Moody Press, 1997)

- *Preaching?*

  by Alec Motyer (Christian Focus Publications, 2013)

- *Walking with the Giants*

  by Warren Wiersbe (Baker Book House, 1976)

- *The Thinker*

  by Roger Carswell (Authentic Media, 2006)

a division of **10** of those.com

10Publishing is the publishing house of **10ofThose**.
It is committed to producing quality Christian
resources that are biblical and accessible.

www.10ofthose.com is our online retail arm selling
thousands of quality books at discounted prices.

For information contact: **info@10ofthose.com**
or check out our website: **www.10ofthose.com**